How to Write
Writing a Letter

by Nick Rebman

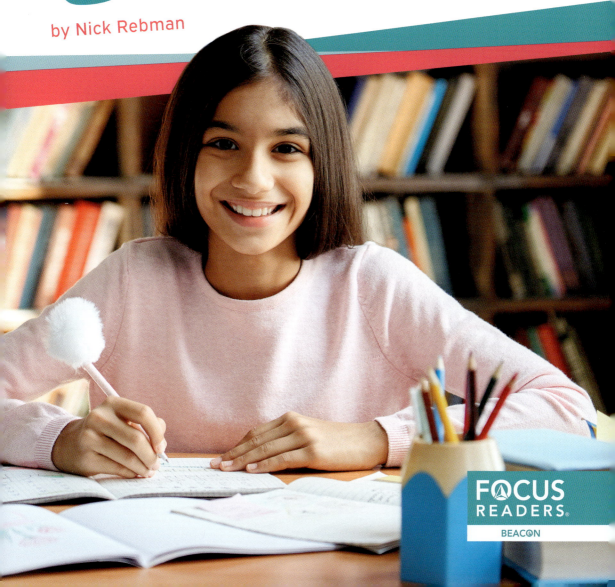

www.focusreaders.com

Copyright © 2024 by Focus Readers®, Mendota Heights, MN 55120. All rights reserved. No part of this book may be reproduced or utilized in any form or by any means without written permission from the publisher.

Focus Readers is distributed by North Star Editions:
sales@northstareditions.com | 888-417-0195

Produced for Focus Readers by Red Line Editorial.

Photographs ©: Shutterstock Images, cover, 1, 7, 19, 20, 23; iStockphoto, 4, 8, 11, 13, 14, 16, 26–27, 29; Red Line Editorial, 25

Library of Congress Cataloging-in-Publication Data
Library of Congress Cataloging-in-Publication Data is available on the Library of Congress website.

ISBN
Names: Rebman, Nick, author.
Title: Writing a letter / by Nick Rebman.
Description: Mendota Heights, MN : Focus Readers, 2024. | Series: How to write | Includes index. | Audience: Grades 2-3
Identifiers: LCCN 2023029415 (print) | LCCN 2023029416 (ebook) | ISBN 9798889980230 (hardcover) | ISBN 9798889980667 (paperback) | ISBN 9798889981497 (pdf) | ISBN 9798889981091 (ebook)
Subjects: LCSH: Letter writing--Juvenile literature. | English language--Composition and exercises--Juvenile literature.
Classification: LCC PE1483 .R34 2024 (print) | LCC PE1483 (ebook) | DDC 808.6--dc23/eng/20230727
LC record available at https://lccn.loc.gov/2023029415
LC ebook record available at https://lccn.loc.gov/2023029416

Printed in the United States of America
Mankato, MN
012024

About the Author

Nick Rebman is a writer and editor who lives in Minnesota.

Table of Contents

CHAPTER 1
Taking Action 5

CHAPTER 2
Reasons to Write 9

CHAPTER 3
Getting Started 15

CHAPTER 4
Parts of a Letter 21

WRITE LIKE A PRO
Editing and Sending 26

Focus on Writing a Letter • 28
Glossary • 30
To Learn More • 31
Index • 32

Chapter 1

Taking Action

A girl is concerned about **climate change**. She knows it is a major problem. And she knows that large actions are needed. So, the girl decides to write a letter to a local lawmaker.

Some people feel anxious about big problems such as climate change. But there are many ways to help.

First, the girl explains her concerns. Her language is polite but firm. She tells the lawmaker that cars are a big part of the problem. She also gives **evidence**. She mentions a report written by scientists.

It's important to use neat handwriting. That way, the reader can easily understand your letter.

 Writing to lawmakers lets them know what issues matter to the people they represent.

Next, the girl asks the lawmaker to take action. She says the city needs more buses and trains. That way, fewer people will use cars. The girl feels hopeful. She believes her letter will help improve her city.

Chapter 2

Reasons to Write

There are many reasons to write letters. Some letters are meant to share feelings. A thank-you note is one example. Suppose someone gave you a gift. Or maybe a friend helped you with a tough problem.

 Many stores sell cards with messages already written. But these cards also have room to write your own letter.

A thank-you note lets the person know you **appreciate** what they did.

A sympathy card also shares feelings. Suppose you know someone in the hospital. Or perhaps your friend's grandfather died. A sympathy card lets the person know you care.

Sometimes people do things they are proud of. When that happens, you can write letters to **congratulate** them.

 Friends and family make parties fun. Invitations let people know they can come.

Other letters share information.

An invitation is one example.

Suppose that your birthday is soon.

You need to tell people a birthday party is happening. You also need to share the party's time and place.

An invitation isn't the only type of letter that shares information. Some letters tell a friend or family member what's new in your life. Suppose you want to tell your uncle what you did during your summer break. A letter is a great way to share this news.

Other letters ask people to take action. Suppose you want a law

 People who live far away often love reading updates from their families.

to change. You could write to a lawmaker. Or perhaps you want your neighbors to take part in a **charity** event. You could write a letter asking them to attend.

13

Chapter 3

Getting Started

Before you start writing, take some time to sit and think. Ask yourself a few questions. For example, who is your letter for? What do you want to say to that person? What is the best way to say it?

 It can take time to decide how you want to write your letter.

 Sometimes your first few ideas don't work. That is okay.

Your **tone** is important. The tone depends on your **audience**. Suppose that you are writing to a lawmaker. In this case, you will use a **formal** tone. Now suppose you're writing to a friend. In this case, you'll use an **informal** tone.

Next, gather your ideas. Make notes of what you want to talk about. You can write the notes on a separate piece of paper. Or you can write them on a computer.

Suppose your new shoe fell apart during a soccer game. So, you are writing to the shoe company. You might make a few notes about this.

One note might be about how you want the company to replace your shoe. One note could describe how it broke. And one note could say how long you've had the shoes.

After that, put your ideas in order. You might start by saying how the shoe broke. That way, the company knows what the problem is. Next,

Did You Know?

The oldest known letter of **complaint** was written more than 3,000 years ago.

 Using numbered lists can help put ideas in order.

you could explain that the shoe wasn't very old. Then, you could end the letter by asking for a new shoe.

19

Chapter 4

Parts of a Letter

Your letter will have several parts. At the top of the page, write the date. This tells the reader when you wrote the letter. Below the date, write your address. Your reader may want to write back.

You can write your letter by hand. Or you can type it on a computer.

The address will let them know where to send their letter.

Next, include a greeting. In a formal letter, you might use *Dear Sir or Madam*. Or you could use *To Whom It May Concern*. In an informal letter, you might use *Dear Grandma* or *Hi, Alex*. Or you could simply use *Hello*. Be sure to put a comma after the greeting.

The body comes next. This is the main part of the letter. It is where you write your message. Make sure

 "Dear" is a common greeting for letters.

the body is in an order that makes sense. You can use words such as *first*, *next*, *then*, and *finally*. These words are called transition words. They help move between ideas.

After the body, include a closing. This shows that the letter is ending. In a formal letter, your closing could be *Sincerely*. An informal letter might use *Love* or *Your Friend*. Add a comma after the closing. On the next line, sign your name.

Did You Know?

Writing an email is similar to writing a letter. But an email has a separate section for the address. Also, the computer adds the date.

A LETTER'S PARTS

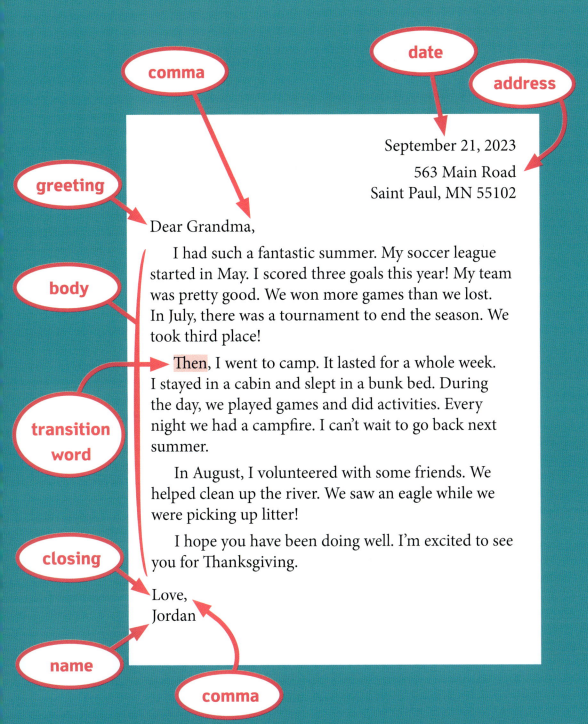

WRITE LIKE A PRO

Editing and Sending

After you finish writing, there is still one more step. Always re-read your letter before sending it. You can make changes as you read. This process is called editing.

It's often helpful to set the letter aside for a while. After that, it will be easier to see any mistakes. Then, you can fix the errors.

Once you're done editing, it is time to send your letter. First, seal it in an envelope. Next, write the person's address on it. Then add a stamp, and put it in a mailbox!

The stamp goes in the top right corner of the envelope.

26

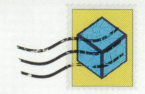

John Doe
123 Main Street, Unit 12
New York City, NY 12345

John Doe
123 Main Street, Unit 12
New York City, NY 12345

FOCUS ON
Writing a Letter

Write your answers on a separate piece of paper.

1. Write a paragraph that explains the main ideas of Chapter 2.

2. Why do you think a formal tone is important when writing to lawmakers?

3. Which type of letter is mainly for sharing feelings?
   - **A.** a thank-you note
   - **B.** a letter to a company
   - **C.** an invitation to a party

4. Suppose you are writing to a family member. What tone would be best?
   - **A.** formal
   - **B.** informal
   - **C.** complaint

5. What does **sympathy** mean in this book?

*A **sympathy** card also shares feelings. Suppose you know someone in the hospital. Or perhaps your friend's grandfather died.*

    A. a person who is old or badly injured
    B. a place where sick people get care
    C. a feeling of sadness for another person

6. What does **errors** mean in this book?

*After that, it will be easier to see any mistakes. Then, you can fix the **errors**.*

    A. things that are correct
    B. things that are wrong
    C. things that are easy to see

Answer key on page 32.

Glossary

appreciate

To be thankful for something.

audience

The person or group a piece of writing is meant for.

charity

Related to helping people in need.

climate change

A human-caused global crisis involving long-term changes in Earth's temperature and weather patterns.

complaint

When a person explains why they're unhappy with something.

congratulate

To tell someone that you are happy for their success.

evidence

Facts or pieces of information that prove something is true.

formal

A style that shows respect and follows rules.

informal

A style that people use in normal, everyday situations.

tone

Manner or style of writing.

To Learn More

BOOKS

Eason, Sarah, and Louise Spilsbury. *How Do I Write Well?* Shrewsbury, UK: Cheriton Children's Books, 2022.

Rajczak Nelson, Kristen. *Letters*. Buffalo, NY: Gareth Stevens Publishing, 2024.

Van Oosbree, Ruthie, and Lauren Kukla. *Free Verse Poems*. Minneapolis: Abdo Publishing, 2023.

NOTE TO EDUCATORS

Visit **www.focusreaders.com** to find lesson plans, activities, links, and other resources related to this title.

Index

A
address, 21–22, 24–25, 26
audience, 16–17

B
body, 22–25

C
closing, 24–25
commas, 22, 24–25

D
date, 21, 24–25

E
editing, 26
email, 24

G
greeting, 22, 25

H
handwriting, 6

I
invitations, 11–12

L
lawmakers, 5–7, 13, 17

N
name, 24–25

S
sympathy cards, 10

T
thank-you notes, 9–10
tone, 16–17
transition words, 23, 25

Answer Key: 1. Answers will vary; **2.** Answers will vary; **3.** A; **4.** B; **5.** C; **6.** B